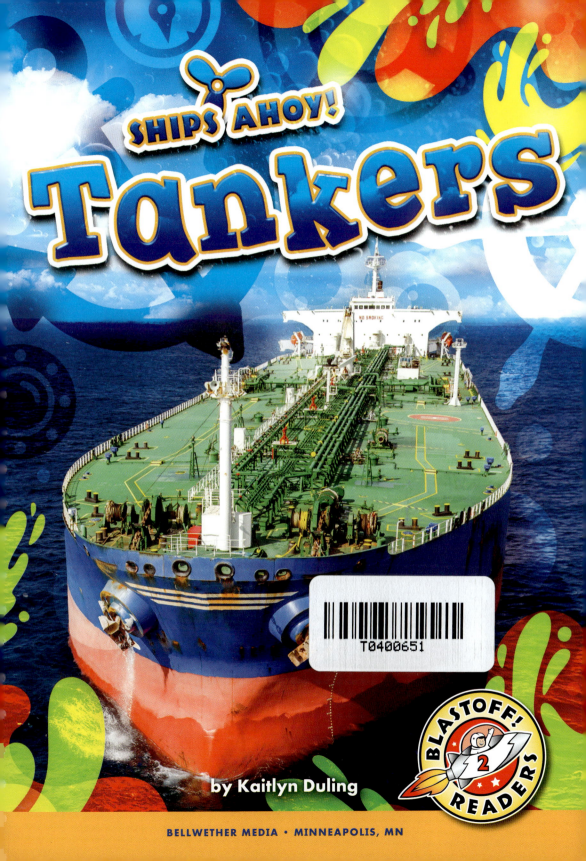

Blastoff! Readers are carefully developed by literacy experts to build reading stamina and move students toward fluency by combining standards-based content with developmentally appropriate text.

 Level 1 provides the most support through repetition of high-frequency words, light text, predictable sentence patterns, and strong visual support.

 Level 2 offers early readers a bit more challenge through varied sentences, increased text load, and text-supportive special features.

 Level 3 advances early-fluent readers toward fluency through increased text load, less reliance on photos, advancing concepts, longer sentences, and more complex special features.

★ **Blastoff! Universe**

Reading Level

 Grade K

 Grades 1–3

 Grade 4

This edition first published in 2026 by Bellwether Media, Inc.

No part of this publication may be reproduced in whole or in part without written permission of the publisher. For information regarding permission, write to Bellwether Media, Inc., Attention: Permissions Department, 3500 American Blvd W, Suite 150, Bloomington, MN 55431.

Library of Congress Cataloging-in-Publication Data

LC record for Tankers available at: https://lccn.loc.gov/2025010684

Text copyright © 2026 by Bellwether Media, Inc. BLASTOFF! READERS and associated logos are trademarks and/or registered trademarks of Bellwether Media, Inc. Bellwether Media is a division of FlutterBee Education Group.

Editor: Suzane Nguyen   Designer: Jeffrey Kollock

Printed in the United States of America, North Mankato, MN.

Table of Contents

What Are Tankers?	4
Tanker Time	12
Go with the Flow	20
Glossary	22
To Learn More	23
Index	24

What Are Tankers?

Tankers are very large ships. They carry **liquids**.

Liquids are stored in **cargo tanks**. They are loaded and unloaded with **pumps**.

Many tankers have a **double hull**. This stops leaks from happening. Leaks are bad for the earth.

Parts of a Tanker

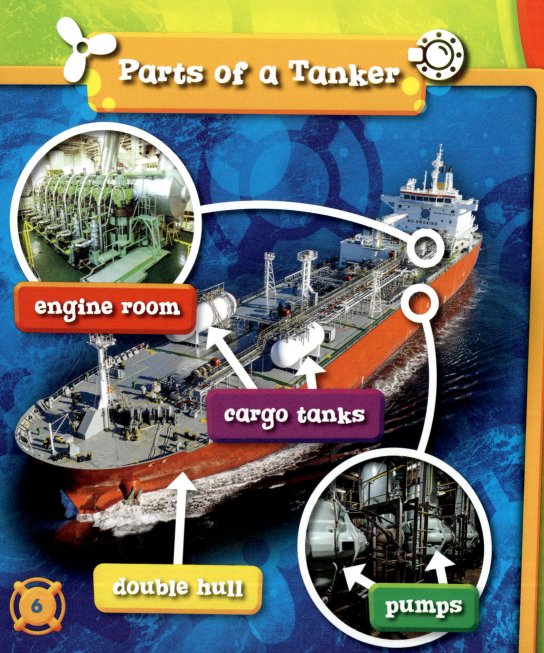

engine room

cargo tanks

double hull

pumps

Big **engines** power tankers. Engines are stored in the engine room.

Edible tankers carry liquids we can eat. Cargo tanks keep the liquids cold. This helps them stay fresh.

Chemical tankers carry liquid chemicals.

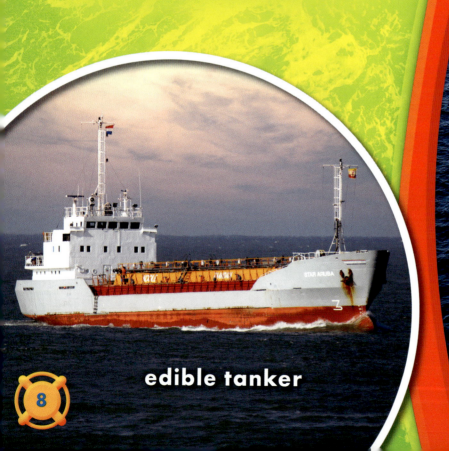

edible tanker

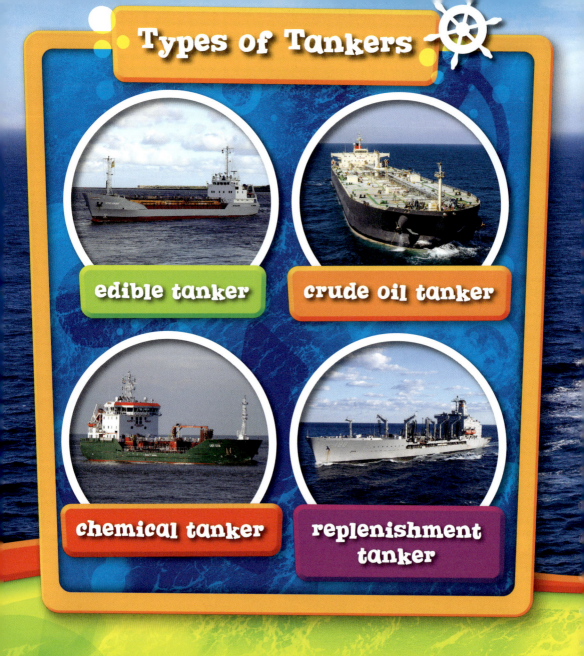

Types of Tankers

edible tanker

crude oil tanker

chemical tanker

replenishment tanker

Crude oil tankers move oil from oceans to land.

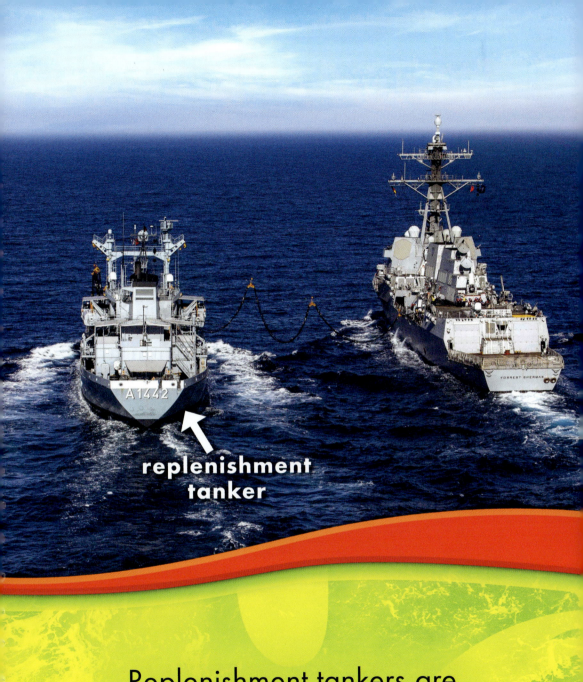

replenishment tanker

Replenishment tankers are used by the **military**. They bring oil to military ships.

Tanker Time

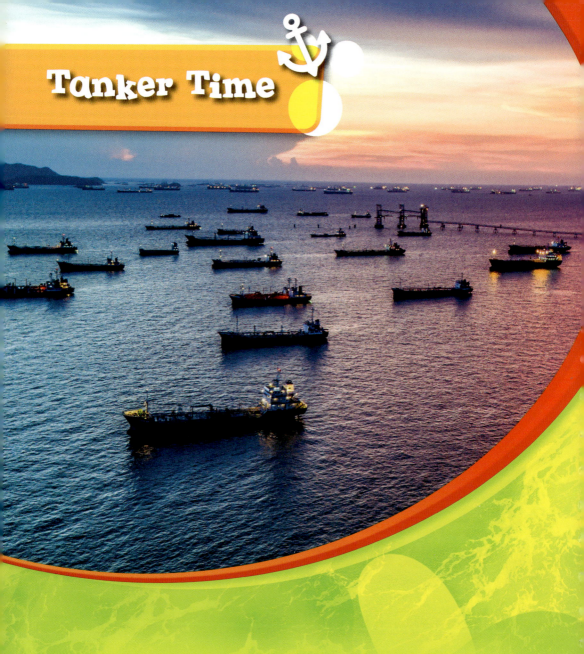

Tankers move liquids around the world. Tanker trips can take weeks or months.

Around 30 people work on tankers.

Ship Stats

USNS John Lewis (T-AO 205)

Size: 746 feet (227.3 meters) long; 106 feet (32.3 meters) wide

Type: replenishment tanker

Top Speed: 20 knots (23 miles or 37 kilometers per hour)

Purpose: brings fuel to U.S. Navy ships and can carry 157,000 barrels of oil

Engineers keep tanker machines running. Tankers can move around 17 **knots** (20 miles or 31 kilometers per hour).

engineer

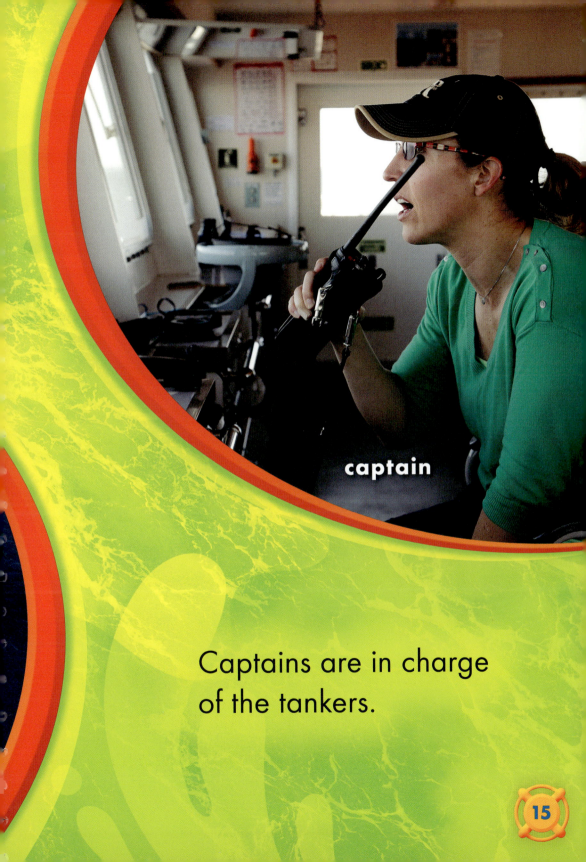

captain

Captains are in charge of the tankers.

Pumpmen fill and empty a ship's tanks at **ports**.

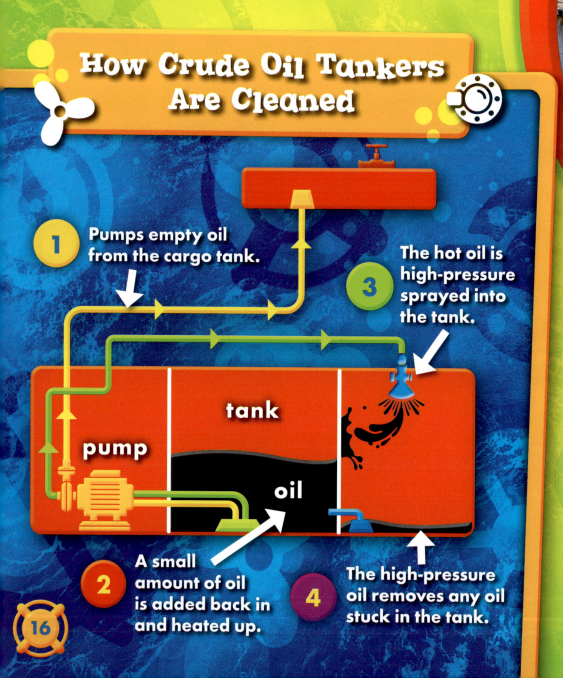

How Crude Oil Tankers Are Cleaned

1. Pumps empty oil from the cargo tank.
2. A small amount of oil is added back in and heated up.
3. The hot oil is high-pressure sprayed into the tank.
4. The high-pressure oil removes any oil stuck in the tank.

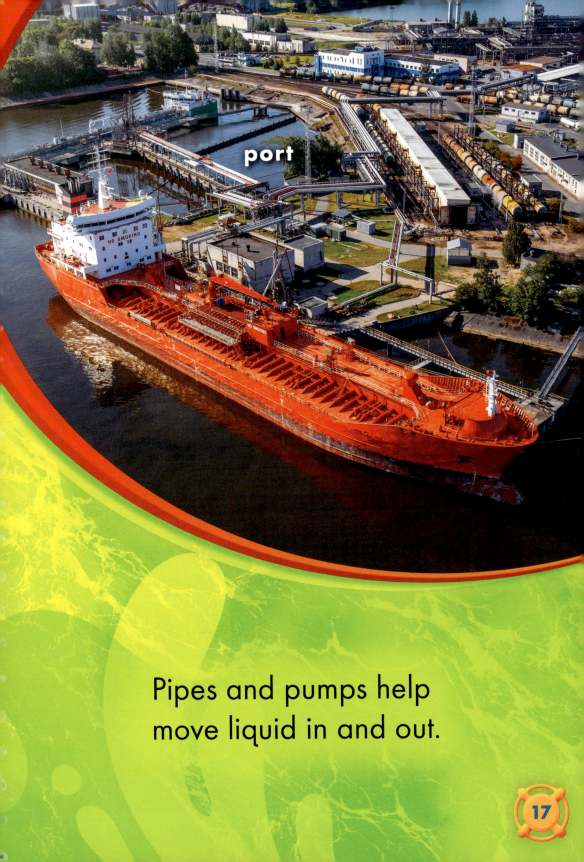

port

Pipes and pumps help move liquid in and out.

oil field

Deck officers talk to workers at **oil fields** and ports.

Cooks work in the ship's **galley**. They feed hungry workers!

galley

Go with the Flow

Without tankers, we would not have liquids like gas for our cars or sweet drinks.

These ships keep liquids flowing all around the world!

Glossary

cargo tanks—large tanks used to carry liquids on ships

chemical—a material that can cause change

crude oil—a yellow-black liquid found underground

double hull—the body of a ship or boat that has two layers

engineers—people who design and build engines, computers, and other machines; engines are parts of machines that make them go.

engines—machines with moving parts that change power into motion

galley—the kitchen on a ship

knots—units of measurement used to explain the speed of a ship

liquids—types of matter that flow and take the shape of their containers

military—the armed forces

oil fields—places on land or on ocean floors where natural gas or oil are found underground

ports—places where ships are loaded and unloaded

pumps—machines that move liquids from one place to another

To Learn More

AT THE LIBRARY
Duling, Kaitlyn. *Container Ships*. Minneapolis, Minn.: Bellwether Media, 2026.

Humphrey, Natalie. *Impressive Drilling Rigs*. New York, N.Y.: Gareth Stevens Publishing, 2023.

Rathburn, Betsy. *A Ship's Day*. Minneapolis, Minn.: Bellwether Media, 2024.

ON THE WEB

FACTSURFER

Factsurfer.com gives you a safe, fun way to find more information.

1. Go to www.factsurfer.com.

2. Enter "tankers" into the search box and click.

3. Select your book cover to see a list of related content.

Index

captains, 15
cargo tanks, 5, 8, 16
chemical tankers, 8, 9
cooks, 19
crude oil tankers, 10, 16
deck officers, 18
double hull, 6, 7
edible tankers, 8
engine room, 7
engineers, 14
engines, 7
galley, 19
how crude oil tankers are cleaned, 16
leaks, 6
liquids, 4, 5, 8, 12, 17, 20
military, 11
oil, 10, 11
oil fields, 18
parts of a tanker, 6
people, 13
ports, 16, 17, 18
pumpmen, 16
pumps, 5, 17
replenishment tankers, 11
speed, 14
trips, 12
types, 10
USNS *John Lewis* (T-AO 205), 13
workers, 18, 19

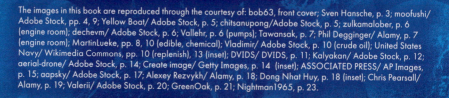

The images in this book are reproduced through the courtesy of: bob63, front cover; Sven Hansche, p. 3; moofushi/ Adobe Stock, pp. 4, 9; Yellow Boat/ Adobe Stock, p. 5; chitsanupong/Adobe Stock, p. 5; zulkamalober, p. 6 (engine room); dechevm/ Adobe Stock, p. 6; Vallehr, p. 6 (pumps); Tawansak, p. 7; Phil Degginger/ Alamy, p. 7 (engine room); MartinLueke, pp. 8, 10 (edible, chemical); Vladimir/ Adobe Stock, p. 10 (crude oil); United States Navy/ Wikimedia Commons, pp. 10 (replenish), 13 (inset); DVIDS/ DVIDS, p. 11; Kalyakan/ Adobe Stock, p. 12; aerial-drone/ Adobe Stock, p. 14; Create image/ Getty Images, p. 14 (inset); ASSOCIATED PRESS/ AP Images, p. 15; aapsky/ Adobe Stock, p. 17; Alexey Rezvykh/ Alamy, p. 18; Dong Nhat Huy, p. 18 (inset); Chris Pearsall/ Alamy, p. 19; Valerii/ Adobe Stock, p. 20; GreenOak, p. 21; Nightman1965, p. 23.